Classic Recipes of
SPAIN

Classic Recipes of
SPAIN

TRADITIONAL FOOD AND COOKING
IN 25 AUTHENTIC DISHES

PEPITA ARIS

LORENZ BOOKS

This edition is published by
Lorenz Books,
an imprint of Anness Publishing Ltd,
Blaby Road, Wigston, LE18 4SE

www.lorenzbooks.com;
www.annesspublishing.com

If you like the images in this book and
would like to investigate using them for
publishing, promotions or advertising,
please visit our website
www.practicalpictures.com for more
information.

Publisher: Joanna Lorenz
Editor: Helen Sudell
Designer: Nigel Partridge
Production Controller: Steve Lang
Recipe Photography: William Lingwood

The image on the front cover is of Seafood
Paella, page 34.

A CIP catalogue record for this book is
available from the British Library

PUBLISHER'S NOTE
Although the advice and information in this
book are believed to be accurate and true
at the time of going to press, neither the
authors nor the publisher can accept any
legal responsibility or liability for any errors
or omissions that may have been made nor
for any inaccuracies nor for any loss, harm
or injury that comes about from following
instructions or advice in this book.

PUBLISHER'S ACKNOWLEDGMENTS
The Publisher would like to thank the
following agencies for the use of their
images. iStockphoto: p6, p10 (both).
Alamy: p9

COOK'S NOTES
Bracketed terms are intended for American
readers. For all recipes, quantities are given
in both metric and imperial measures and,
where appropriate, in standard cups and
spoons. Follow one set of measures, but
not a mixture, because they are not
interchangeable.

Standard spoon and cup measures are
level. 1 tsp = 5ml, 1 tbsp = 15ml, 1 cup =
250ml/8fl oz. Australian standard
tablespoons are 20ml. Australian readers
should use 3 tsp in place of 1 tbsp for
measuring small quantities.

American pints are 16fl oz/2 cups.
American readers should use 20fl oz/2.5
cups in place of 1 pint when measuring
liquids.

Electric oven temperatures in this book are
for conventional ovens. When using a fan
oven, the temperature will probably need to
be reduced by about 10–20°C/20–40°F.
Since ovens vary, you should check with
your manufacturer's instruction book for
guidance.

The nutritional analysis given for each
recipe is calculated per portion (i.e. serving
or item), unless otherwise stated. If the
recipe gives a range, such as Serves 4–6,
then the nutritional analysis will be for the
smaller portion size, i.e. 6 servings. The
analysis does not include optional
ingredients, such as salt added to taste.

Medium (US large) eggs are used unless
otherwise stated.

Contents

Introduction

The history and religion of Spain are visible on the plate. The old adage that we are what we eat is particularly relevant to this Mediterranean country. Ingredients, cooking methods and classic recipes all have an easy-to-trace and fascinating past. The Moors, Jews and Catholics have contributed cooking styles and flavours that still survive today, and the introduction of new foods from America brought exciting influences to the Mediterranean diet. Throughout these cultural upheavals the Spanish way of combining fresh food with simple herbs and spices to achieve maximum taste has remained at the heart of their diverse and rich cuisine.

Left: Ancient olive groves are a familiar part of the Spanish landscape.

Spanish Cuisine

The Spanish are a gregarious people and much of their social life revolves around food. Many people breakfast in a bar before going to work. They can enjoy *café con leche* and *tostadas* (toast) or if they are not in a hurry there is always hot chocolate with churros – long strips of deep fried batter for dunking in the hot chocolate.

Lunch is a big affair, with either meat or fish as the main dish accompanied with

Below: Churros dipped into piping hot chocolate are a favourite treat.

Above: A small bowl of olives, pickled cucumbers and fish rolls is typical tapas fare.

vegetables. Children have a *merienda* (drink and snack) after school. Women may meet friends for a merienda after work, while men enjoy an *aperitivo*. Whole families go for the *paseo* – a seven o'clock promenade when the sun has lost its intensity. Supper is late, and is a light meal, often vegetable-based.

Home cooking

The Spanish have a passion for slow-cooking, which can go on all day with the aroma of a large pot of mixed pulses, meats and

sausages wafting around the house. Eating outdoors is part of the Spanish psyche and houses have balconies and patios with built-in charcoal barbecues to make the most of the long summer days. The Spanish are also great picnickers and delight in family gatherings where a large paella is cooked.

Tapas

Spain's greatest food invention, the humble tapas, started out as a simple piece of bread, soon topped with ham or cheese, balanced over a glass to keep out the flies – the word *tapa* means a cover. It is not meant to be a meal. The idea is that each person chooses one or two tapa dishes to accompany a drink. In this way everyone gets to share. As with most traditional Spanish cooking, Tapas food is really authentic – good local ingredients presented with flair.

Right: Cooking a large pot of paella outside is an age-old tradition in Spain.

Spanish Food and Festivals

In Spain, almost every event involves food. There are special foods for feast days – and feast days solely to celebrate food. Holy week is an occasion of high drama but the local saint's day, or an incident in the town's history, will be celebrated with processions and plenty to eat.

Christmas

Spaniards tend to eat a meal after going to church on Christmas Eve. You will be served salt cod cream (*bacalao al arriero*) in Aragón, *lubina* (sea bream) and red cabbage in Madrid, and roast turkey if you

Below: Turrón *(almond nougat) is a popular Christmas treat.*

are Catalan. There are gifts of almond turrón and marzipan handed out to the children.

Holy week

Semana Santa, the period in between Palm Sunday and Easter, is the big festival, particularly in the south. The heavy *pasos* (scenes of Christ's death) and the weeping virgins banked by scented lilies and tall candles are paraded night after night.The Easter foods are few: *torijillos* (sweet fried toast), cheesecake, and perhaps lamb for *Resurreción* day.

Celebrating the seasons

Food coming into season is joyfully greeted, for example, the reappearance of freshwater crayfish, or the first salmon of the year. In Murcia, the end of Lent is marked with floats and a parade for the 'Burial of the Sardine'. The return of sardines to Spanish waters marks the coming of summer. Fishermen give thanks to San Pedro and the Virgen de Carmen on 15 July with large fish suppers.

Above: A Tarta de Santiago *displaying St James' sword.*

Saints' days and patronal festivals

Spaniards don't have birthdays but instead celebrate their saint's day where flowers and candies are handed out to the children bearing that name. Towns also seek the protection of a saint, whose image is paraded annually. These days are a frenzy of baking.

In Badajoz, people celebrate with little Moorish fritters, and in Logroño they eat yeast buns called *bollas* for San Marco. To celebrate San José on 19 March, everyone eats *buñuelos de viento*, little choux puffs that "just blow away". In Madrid these airy pastries are made with lard and cogñac, and have a special filling of rich, sweet, creamy custard to celebrate San Isidro.

St James' day

Spain's National Day on 25 July means fiesta time in Santiago de Compostela. Crowds gather around the cathedral and bars serve octopus *a al feria*, gently stewed with paprika. There is also grilled lobster followed by *tarta de Santiago*, a cinnamon

almond tart decorated with a stencil of St James' great two-handed sword outlined in powdered sugar.

Matanza – pig killing time

The matanza is the biggest social festival of the year. November is traditionally the time to kill the pig and make sausages. The annual event brings families together and lasts for two or more days. The pig's liver, cooked with onions, is served for lunch on the first day, and the kidneys with rice and potatoes on the second.

Above: Panellets are eaten at the All Saints Day festivals.

Day of the dead

All Saints, on 1 November, is celebrated by families all over Spain. Flowers are carried to graveyards and *Huesos de santos* (saints' bones), made of almond pastry, sweet potato or batter, are eaten. Sometimes they are fried around a bamboo cane, making them ghoulishly hollow. Catalans bake little nut *panellets* (cookies). In Galicia, there are all-night vigils, with chestnuts roasting on braziers.

Below: The classic chorizo sausage, flavoured with paprika.

Classic Ingredients

The wonderful ingredients of Spain – olives, rice, vegetables, cheeses, sausages, and fish and shellfish from the longest coastline in Europe – have shaped the country's individual style of cooking. These ingredients are matched by cooking methods and recipes that best display their virtues.

Game birds and meat

The Spanish countryside is full of wildlife, and out in the country the sign *coto de caza* (shooting reserve) is a constant reminder that hunting is a passion. Pigeon, partridge and quail are the most commonly eaten game

Below: Serrano ham is one of the finest cured meats.

birds, often in cooked rich casseroles with earthy mushrooms, garlic and wine.

The Spanish have never been great beef eaters as the hot temperatures mean that cattle are not reared throughout the country. Meatballs are, however, sold in every bar and cuts such as salt brisket go into stews. Despite being an expensive meat in Spain, lamb is still the traditional meat in the grazing regions of central and western Spain. Elsewhere, it is an Easter or wedding treat. Pork is the favoured meat in Spain and although cured meat is eaten more often than fresh, pork chops and loin of pork remain Spain's most familiar meat. Pork is delicious *a la trianera* (roasted with sherry); *Magro* is a pork steak commonly served with a tomato sauce; and *cochefrito* is chopped fried meat flavoured with vinegar and paprika. Other cuts of pork are cured, including the ubiquitous ham. Finally, any pork that isn't used as fresh meat is turned into sausages. The raw pork is minced

(ground), or hand chopped, mixed with back fat and spices, then stuffed into casings. The bigger the pieces of meat, and the lower the fat content, the sweeter the meat is.

Fish and seafood

The two coasts of Spain provide a multitude of fish. The most popular everyday fish are cod, *pescadilla* (a small hake) and small flat fish such as *gallo* (a type of plaice). For special occasions, luxury fish such as sea bass, turbot and monkfish are cooked in wine and shellfish sauces, or with cider and boiled potatoes.

The Spanish adore preserved fish and *bacalao* (salt cod) is still weekly fare across the country. Other fish are salted too, including sardines and anchovies.

Spanish shellfish is among the finest in the world and is cooked either boiled or *la parrilla* (on the barbecue) served with sea salt and lemon wedges.

Right: Sardines are a popular fish, eaten throughout Spain.

Above: Table olives are served with aperitivo *in many bars.*

Olives and olive oil

One of the oldest Mediterranean crops, the olive tree is thought to have been spread throughout Spain by the Phoenicians before 1000BC. Spanish olives are mainly picked when they are bright green and unripe. They are washed several times to remove the bitterness and then stored in brine with flavours added. Pitted olives stuffed with little pieces of cooked pimiento, slivers of almond, anchovy or roasted garlic are also sold.

The oil made from these olives is exported around the world and is typically rich and fruity with an olive aroma.

Cheese and dairy

Spain produces about 200 varieties of cheese, most of them in farmhouse dairies, the hard cheeses being the most successful. Manchego is Spain's premier cheese, made from the milk of Manchega ewes. Golden inside, it becomes stronger as it ages.

In the south of the country cheeses are predominantly made with goat's milk. Their flavour is distinct and clean, not so pungent as many of the French varieties, and they have a light, crumbly texture.

Spain is a country of poultry breeders and the use of eggs in cooking reflects this. Galician free-range (farm-fresh) eggs are famous for the red albumen in their yolks – they are used in Madrid for making tortillas.

Rice and pasta

These two staples are at the heart of both everyday meals and classic celebration dishes in Spain. Rice is eaten on a daily basis in the east and south of the country. It is eaten plain,

Above: Manchego is a Spanish hard cheese.

added to soupy stews, and combined with beans to make stuffings for vegetables. Many dessert puddings contain rice and *Arroz con leche* (rice pudding) rivals *flan* (baked custard) as Spain's national dessert. Rice is also the main ingredient in paella, which is cooked all over Spain, at picnics and family celebrations, in a flat pan set over a charcoal fire. Other paella ingredients include rabbit, chicken or shellfish.

Pasta has been eaten in Spain for longer than it has in northern Italy. *Fideos*, a short spaghetti is used in soups and is combined with shellfish to make a similar,

Above: Bomba is the most popular variety of paella rice.

but easier, dish to paella. Flat dry squares of pasta are also sold for making lasagne or for rolling into *canelones* (cannelloni).

Vegetables
The Spanish are blessed with richly fertile soil in which to grow a wide variety of summer and winter vegetables. In spring, fresh peas, green beans, asparagus and shoots of garlic are gathered together and served in egg dishes and *menestras* (vegetable stews).

The Moors introduced spinach and their beloved aubergine (eggplant), which are both cooked with pine nuts, garlic and cheese. The Moors also loved onions,

especially raw. Garlic is integral to Spanish cuisine and is usually the first ingredient into the frying pan. It is used to flavour the oil, but is then often discarded before adding the rest of the ingredients.

The Mediterranean climate is ideal for growing tomatoes, chillies, (bell) peppers, courgettes (zucchini) and potatoes. All have become staple ingredients in the Spanish kitchen.

Fruits
With such a hot climate, fruit is grown the length and breadth of the country. The apricot trees are the first to flower in spring, but it is apples that are grown across

Below: Spanish onions are mild enough to be eaten raw.

Above: Citrus fruits are exported from Spain around the world.

Spain. Peaches, plums, pears and cherries are widely available, and quinces are made into a delicious orange paste (*membrillo*), which is often served with cheese.

Golden grapes drape across vineyards in the south, and the coast from Alicante to Valencia is famous for fat, juicy muscats. Melons, strawberries and figs are also highly prized.

It was the Moors that first planted orange trees in Spain and the juice was squeezed over fish – and still is – in the way that we now use lemons. Limes, lemons and grapefruit are also widely used, with citrus fruit being exported to many other countries.

Tastes of the Mediterranean

Spanish food and cooking is renowned for its fantastic flavours, vibrant fresh ingredients and regional differences. It is as rich and diverse as the landscape itself, and reflects its people's history, traditions and way of life. From moreish tapas such as Patatas Bravas and Pinchito Moruños to the classic Paella Valencia, and from the national meat dish Cocido to irresistible desserts like Crema Catalana and crunchy Panellets, the recipes presented here are from all over Spain and represent the very best of its wonderful culinary heritage.

Left: Fresh, local ingredients are key to the success of Spanish home cooking.

Olive and Anchovy Bites
Oliva y Anchoas Galettas

Makes 40–45

115g/4oz/1 cup plain (all-purpose)
    flour, plus extra for dusting
115g/4oz/½ cup chilled butter, diced
115g/4oz/1 cup finely grated
    Manchego, mature (sharp)
    Cheddar or Gruyère cheese
50g/2oz can anchovy fillets in oil,
    drained and roughly chopped
50g/2oz/½ cup pitted black olives,
    roughly chopped
2.5ml/½ tsp cayenne pepper
sea salt, to serve

1 Place the flour, butter, cheese, anchovies, olives and cayenne pepper in a food processor and pulse until the mixture forms a firm dough.

2 Wrap the dough loosely in clear film (plastic wrap). Chill for 20 minutes.

3 Preheat the oven to 200°C/400°F/Gas 6. Roll out the dough thinly on a lightly floured surface.

4 Cut the dough into 5cm/2in wide strips, then cut across each strip in alternate directions, to make triangles. Transfer to baking sheets and bake for 8–10 minutes until golden. Cool on a wire rack. Sprinkle with sea salt.

These little melt-in-the-mouth morsels are made from two ingredients that are forever associated with tapas – olives and anchovies. The reason for this is that both contain salt, which helps to stimulate thirst and therefore drinking.

Beetroot Crisps
Remolacha Fritas

Serves 4

1 small fresh beetroot (beet)
caster (superfine) sugar and fine salt,
    for sprinkling
olive oil, for frying
coarse sea salt and garlic
    mayonnaise, to serve

The Spanish love new and colourful snacks. Try these vibrant crisps (US potato chips), which make an appealing alternative to potato crisps. Serve them with a bowl of creamy, garlic mayonnaise, and use the crisps to scoop up the dip.

1 Peel the beetroot and, using a mandolin or a vegetable peeler, cut it into very thin slices.

2 Lay the slices on kitchen paper and lightly sprinkle them with sugar and fine salt.

3 Heat 5cm/2in oil in a deep pan until a bread cube turns golden in 1 minute. Cook the slices in batches, until they float to the surface and turn golden at the edge. Drain on kitchen paper and sprinkle with sea salt when cool.

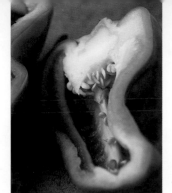

Potatoes in Spicy Sauce
Patatas Bravas

1 Scrub the potatoes and put them into a pan of salted water. Bring to the boil and cook for 10 minutes, or until almost tender. Drain and leave to cool slightly. Peel, if you like, then cut into chunks.

2 Heat the oil in a large frying or sauté pan and fry the potatoes, turning them frequently, until golden.

3 Meanwhile, crush together the garlic, chillies and cumin using a mortar and pestle. Mix the paste with the paprika and wine vinegar, then add to the potatoes with the sliced pepper and cook, stirring, for 2 minutes. Scatter with salt, if using, and serve hot as a tapas dish or cold as a side dish.

Serves 4
675g/1½lb small new potatoes
75ml/5 tbsp olive oil
2 garlic cloves, sliced
3 dried chillies, seeded and chopped
2.5ml/½ tsp ground cumin
10ml/2 tsp paprika
30ml/2 tbsp red or white wine
   vinegar
1 red or green (bell) pepper, seeded
   and sliced
coarse sea salt, for sprinkling
   (optional)

There are several variations on this chilli and potato dish, but the most important thing is the spicing, which is made hotter still by adding vinegar. The classic version is made with fresh tomato sauce flavoured with garlic and chilli. The name bravas *implies that the potatoes are so hot that you have to be extremely brave to eat them.*

Garlic Prawns
Gambas al Ajillo

Serves 4

1–2 dried chillies (to taste)
60ml/4 tbsp olive oil
3 garlic cloves, finely chopped
16 large raw prawns (shrimp),
    in the shell
salt and ground black pepper
crusty bread, to serve

Garlic prawns are hugely popular in Spain, both with and without the addition of chilli. They are normally cooked in small, individual earthenware casseroles, which stand on an iron baking sheet – la plancha. A frying pan will produce the same result.

1 Split the chillies lengthways and discard the seeds. It is best to do this with a knife and fork, because the seeds, in particular, contain hot capsicum, which can be very irritating to the eyes, nose and mouth.

2 Heat the oil in a large frying pan and stir-fry the garlic and chilli for 1 minute, until the garlic begins to turn brown.

3 Add the whole prawns and stir-fry for 3–4 minutes, coating them well with the flavoured oil.

4 Remove from the heat and divide the prawns among four dishes. Spoon over the flavoured oil and serve immediately with plenty of bread to soak up the juices. (Remember to provide a plate for the heads and shells, plus plenty of napkins for messy fingers.)

Moorish Skewers
Pinchitos Moruños

Serves 4

2.5ml/½ tsp cumin seeds
2.5ml/½ tsp coriander seeds
2 garlic cloves, finely chopped
5ml/1 tsp paprika
2.5ml/½ tsp dried oregano
15ml/1 tbsp lemon juice
45ml/3 tbsp olive oil
500g/1¼lb lean pork
salt and ground black pepper

1 Starting a couple of hours in advance, grind the cumin and coriander seeds in a mortar and work in the garlic with a pinch of salt. Add the paprika and oregano and mix in the lemon juice. Stir in the oil.

2 Cut the pork into small cubes, then skewer them, three or four at a time, on to cocktail sticks (toothpicks). Put the skewered meat in a shallow dish, and pour over the marinade. Spoon the marinade back over the meat to ensure it is well coated. Leave to marinate in a cool place for 2 hours.

3 Preheat the grill (broiler) to high, and line the grill pan with foil. Spread the kebabs out in a row and place under the grill, close to the heat. Cook for about 3 minutes on each side, spooning the juices over when you turn them, until cooked through. Sprinkle with salt and pepper, and serve at once.

The Moors introduced both skewers and marinated meat to Spain. These little yellow kebabs are a favourite in Andalusia, where many butchers sell the meat ready-marinated. The Arab versions used lamb, but pork is preferred now, because the spicing fits so perfectly.

Spicy Sausage and Cheese Tortilla
Tortilla de Queso y Chorizo

Serves 4–6

75ml/5 tbsp olive oil

175g/6oz frying chorizo or spicy sausage, thinly sliced

675g/1½lb waxy potatoes, thinly sliced

2 Spanish onions, halved and thinly sliced

4 large (US extra large) eggs

30ml/2 tbsp chopped fresh parsley, plus extra to garnish

115g/4oz/1 cup grated Cheddar or other hard cheese

salt and ground black pepper

1 Heat 15ml/1 tbsp of the oil in a 20cm/8in non-stick frying pan and fry the sausage until golden brown and cooked through. Lift out with a slotted spoon and drain on kitchen paper.

2 Add a further 30ml/2 tbsp oil to the pan and fry the potatoes and onions for 2–3 minutes, turning frequently (the pan will be very full). Cover tightly and cook over a gentle heat for about 30 minutes, turning occasionally, until softened and slightly golden.

3 In a large mixing bowl, beat together the eggs, parsley, cheese, sausage and plenty of seasoning. Gently stir in the potatoes and onions until coated, taking care not to break up the potato too much.

4 Wipe out the pan with kitchen paper and heat the remaining 30ml/ 2 tbsp oil. Add the potato mixture and cook, over a very low heat, until the egg begins to set. Use a metal spatula to prevent the tortilla from sticking and allow the uncooked egg to run underneath.

5 Preheat the grill (broiler) to high. When the base of the tortilla has set, which should take about 5 minutes, protect the pan handle with foil and place the tortilla under the grill until it is set and golden. Cut into wedges and serve garnished with parsley.

This substantial tortilla is delicious hot or cold. Cut it into chunky wedges and serve for supper or a light lunch with a fresh tomato and basil salad. The addition of spicy chorizo and tangy cheese gives it a wonderful, rich flavour.

Chilled Tomato and Garlic Soup
Gazpacho

Serves 4

1.3–1.6kg/3–3½lb ripe tomatoes
1 green (bell) pepper, seeded and
    roughly chopped
2 garlic cloves, finely chopped
2 slices stale bread, crusts removed
60ml/4 tbsp extra virgin olive oil
60ml/4 tbsp sherry vinegar
150ml/¼ pint/⅔ cup tomato juice
300ml/½ pint/1¼ cups iced water
salt and ground black pepper
ice cubes, to serve (optional)

For the garnishes

30ml/2 tbsp olive oil
2–3 slices stale bread, diced
1 small cucumber, peeled
    and finely diced
1 small onion, finely chopped
1 red (bell) and 1 green (bell) pepper,
    seeded and finely diced
2 hard-boiled eggs, chopped

*This classic chilled soup is
deeply rooted in Andalusia.
Serving it with saucerfuls
of garnishes has become
a tradition.*

1 Skin the tomatoes, then quarter them and remove the cores and seeds, saving the juices. Put the pepper in a food processor and process for a few seconds. Add the tomatoes, reserved juices, garlic, bread, oil and vinegar and process. Add the tomato juice and blend to combine.

2 Season the soup, then pour into a large bowl, cover with clear film (plastic wrap) and chill for at least 12 hours.

3 Prepare the garnishes. Heat the olive oil in a frying pan and fry the bread cubes for 4–5 minutes until golden brown and crisp. Drain well on kitchen paper, then arrange in a small dish. Place each of the remaining garnishes in separate small dishes.

4 Just before serving, dilute the soup with the ice-cold water. The consistency should be thick but not too stodgy. If you like, stir a few ice cubes into the soup, then spoon into serving bowls and serve with the prepared garnishes.

Sherried Onion Soup with Saffron
Sopa de Cebolla con Jerez y Azafrán

Serves 4

40g/1½oz/3 tbsp butter
2 large yellow onions, thinly sliced
1 small garlic clove, finely chopped
pinch of saffron threads (0.05g)
50g/2oz blanched almonds, toasted
    and finely ground
750ml/1¼ pints/3 cups chicken
    or vegetable stock
45ml/3 tbsp fino sherry
2.5ml/½ tsp paprika
salt and ground black pepper

To garnish

30ml/2 tbsp flaked or slivered
    almonds, toasted
chopped fresh parsley

The Spanish combination of onions, sherry and saffron gives this pale yellow soup a beguiling taste that is perfect for the opening course of a meal. The addition of ground almonds to thicken the soup gives it a wonderful flavour.

1 Melt the butter in a heavy pan over a low heat. Add the onions and garlic, then cover the pan and cook very gently, stirring frequently, for about 20 minutes, or until the onions are soft and golden yellow.

2 Add the saffron threads to the pan and cook, uncovered, for 3–4 minutes, then add the finely ground almonds and cook, stirring the ingredients constantly, for a further 2–3 minutes.

3 Pour the chicken or vegetable stock and sherry into the pan and stir in 5ml/1 tsp salt and the paprika. Season with black pepper. Bring to the boil, then lower the heat and simmer gently for about 10 minutes.

4 Pour the soup into a food processor and process until smooth, then return it to the rinsed pan. Reheat slowly, stirring occasionally. Taste for seasoning, adding more salt and pepper if required.

5 Ladle the soup into heated bowls, garnish with the toasted almonds and a little chopped fresh parsley and serve immediately.

Seafood Soup
Sopa de Mariscos

1 Pull the heads off the prawns and put them in a pan with the cold water. Add the onion, celery and bay leaf and simmer for 20–25 minutes.

2 Peel the prawns, adding the shells to the stock as you go along.

3 Heat the oil in a wide, deep flameproof casserole and fry the bread slices quickly, then reserve them. Fry the onion until it is soft, adding the garlic towards the end.

4 Scoop the seeds out of the tomatoes and discard. Chop the flesh and add to the casserole with the green pepper. Fry briefly, stirring occasionally.

5 Strain the stock into the casserole and bring to the boil. Check over the cockles or mussels, discarding any that are open or damaged.

6 Add half the cockles or mussels to the stock. When open, use a slotted spoon to transfer some of them out on to a plate. Remove the mussels or cockles from the shells and discard the shells. (You should end up having discarded about half of the shells.) Meanwhile, repeat the process to cook the remaining cockles or mussels.

7 Return the cockles or mussels to the soup and add the prawns. Add the bread, and the lemon juice and chopped parsley.

8 Season to taste with paprika, salt and pepper and stir gently to dissolve the bread. Serve at once, providing a plate for the empty shells.

This hearty seafood soup contains all the colours and flavours of the Mediterranean. It is substantial enough to serve as a main course, but can also be diluted with a little white wine and water, to make an elegant appetizer for six.

Serves 4

675g/1½lb raw prawns (shrimp), in the shell
900ml/1½ pints/3¾ cups cold water
1 onion, chopped
1 celery stick, chopped
1 bay leaf
45ml/3 tbsp olive oil
2 slices stale bread, crusts removed and torn into little pieces
1 small onion, finely chopped
1 large garlic clove, chopped
2 large tomatoes, halved
½ large green (bell) pepper, finely chopped
500g/1¼lb cockles (small clams) or mussels, cleaned*
juice of 1 lemon
45ml/3 tbsp chopped fresh parsley
5ml/1 tsp paprika
salt and ground black pepper

*Discard any mussels or clams that are not closed prior to cooking.

Roast Peppers and Onions
Mojete

1 Halve the peppers and remove the seeds. Cut each pepper lengthways into 12 strips. Preheat the oven to 200°C/400°F/Gas 6.

2 Place the peppers, onion, garlic, black olives and tomatoes in a large roasting pan.

3 Sprinkle the vegetables with the sugar, then pour in the sherry. Season well with salt and pepper, cover with foil and bake for 45 minutes.

4 Remove the foil from the pan and stir the mixture well. Add the rosemary sprigs and drizzle with the olive oil. Return the pan to the oven and cook for a further 30 minutes, uncovered, until the vegetables are very tender. Serve hot or cold with plenty of chunks of fresh crusty bread.

COOK'S TIP
Spain is the world's chief olive producer, with half the crop being exported. Try to use good quality Spanish olives for this recipe. Choose unpitted ones as they have a better flavour.

Serves 8
2 red (bell) peppers
2 yellow (bell) peppers
1 red onion, sliced
2 garlic cloves, halved
50g/2oz/¼ cup black olives
6 large ripe tomatoes, quartered
5ml/1 tsp soft light brown sugar
45ml/3 tbsp amontillado sherry
3–4 fresh rosemary sprigs
30ml/2 tbsp olive oil
salt and ground black pepper
crusty bread, to serve

The Spanish love to scoop up cooked vegetables with bread, and the name of this dish, which is derived from the word meaning to dip, reflects that. Peppers, tomatoes and onions are baked together to make a colourful, soft vegetable dish that is studded with olives. In the summer the vegetables can be cooked on the barbecue.

Broad Beans with Bacon
Habas y Jamón

Serves 4

30ml/2 tbsp olive oil
1 small onion, finely chopped
1 garlic clove, finely chopped
50g/2oz rindless smoked streaky
    (fatty) bacon, roughly chopped
225g/8oz broad (fava) beans, thawed
    if frozen
5ml/1 tsp paprika
15ml/1 tbsp sweet sherry
salt and ground black pepper

This dish is particularly associated with Ronda, in southern Spain, the home of bull fighting, where broad beans are fed to fighting bulls to build them up. It is also found elsewhere in Spain where it is known as habas españolas. *If you have time, remove the dull skins from the broad beans to reveal the bright green beans beneath.*

1 Heat the olive oil in a large frying pan or sauté pan. Add the chopped onion, garlic and bacon and fry over a high heat for about 5 minutes, stirring frequently, until the onion is softened and the bacon browned.

2 Add the beans and paprika to the pan and stir-fry for 1 minute. Add the sherry, lower the heat, cover and cook for 5–10 minutes until the beans are tender. Season with salt and pepper to taste and serve hot or warm.

VARIATION
For a vegetarian version of this dish use sun-dried tomatoes in oil instead of bacon.

Lentils with Mushrooms and Anis
Lentejas con Champiñones y Anis

Serves 4

30ml/2 tbsp olive oil
1 large onion, sliced
2 garlic cloves, finely chopped
250g/9oz/3 cups brown cap (cremini)
  mushrooms, sliced
150g/5oz/generous ½ cup brown
  or green lentils, soaked overnight
4 tomatoes, cut in eighths
1 bay leaf
25g/1oz/½ cup chopped fresh
  parsley
30ml/2 tbsp anis spirit or anisette
salt, paprika and black pepper

1 Heat the oil in a flameproof casserole. Add the onion and fry gently, with the garlic, until softened but not browned.

2 Add the sliced mushrooms and stir to combine with the onion and garlic. Continue cooking, stirring gently, for a couple of minutes.

3 Add the lentils, tomatoes and bay leaf with 175ml/6fl oz/¾ cup water. Simmer gently, covered, for 30–40 minutes until the lentils are soft, and the liquid has almost disappeared.

4 Stir in the parsley and anis. Season with salt, paprika and black pepper.

COOK'S TIP
If you forget to soak the lentils, add an additional 30 minutes to the cooking time.

The great plains of Castile produce lentils for the whole of Europe. Locally they are weekly fare. In this recipe, lentejas con champiñones, they are flavoured with another product of the region, anis spirit, plus a great deal of parsley. Serve this dish on its own, or with grilled pork.

Seafood Paella
Paella con Mariscos

Serves 4

45ml/3 tbsp olive oil
1 Spanish onion, chopped
2 large garlic cloves, chopped
150g/5oz frying chorizo, sliced
300g/11oz small squid, cleaned
1 red (bell) pepper, cut into strips
4 tomatoes, peeled, seeded and
    diced or 200g/7oz can tomatoes
500ml/17fl oz/2¼ cups chicken
    stock, plus a little extra
105ml/7 tbsp dry white wine
200g/7oz/1 cup paella rice
pinch of saffron threads (0.2g),
    crumbled
150g/5oz/generous 1 cup peas
12 large cooked prawns (shrimp),
    in the shell or 8 peeled scampi
    (extra large shrimp)
450g/1lb fresh mussels, scrubbed*
450g/1lb clams, scrubbed*
4 cooked king prawns (jumbo shrimp)
    or scampi, in the shells
salt and ground black pepper
chopped fresh parsley and lemon
    wedges, to garnish

*Discard any mussels or clams that
are not closed prior to cooking.

1 Heat the olive oil in a paella pan or large frying pan, add the onion and garlic and fry until translucent. Add the chorizo and fry until lightly golden.

2 If the squid are very small, leave them whole, otherwise cut the bodies into rings and the tentacles into pieces. Add the squid to the pan and sauté over a high heat for 2 minutes.

3 Stir in the pepper and tomatoes and simmer gently for 5 minutes, until the pepper is tender. Pour in the stock and wine, stir well and bring to the boil. Stir in the rice and saffron and season well. Spread the contents evenly over the base of the pan. Bring the liquid back to the boil, then lower the heat and simmer for about 10 minutes.

4 Gently stir the peas, prawns or scampi, mussels and clams into the rice, then cook for a further 15–20 minutes, until the rice is tender and all the mussels and clams have opened. (Discard any that remain closed.) If the paella seems dry, stir in a little more hot stock.

5 Remove the pan from the heat and arrange the king prawns or scampi on top. Cover and leave to stand for 5 minutes. Sprinkle the paella with chopped parsley and serve straight from the pan, accompanied by lemon wedges.

This is a great dish to serve to guests on a special occasion. A seafood paella always looks spectacular and a bed of scented rice is the perfect way to display a selection of mariscos (seafood). This particular paella contains a magnificent combination of squid, prawns, mussels and clams as well as spicy chorizo and succulent vegetables.

Scallops in Tomato Sauce
Vieiras de Santiago

1 Heat the oil in a pan and fry the onion and garlic over a gentle heat. Add the tomatoes and cook for 10–15 minutes, stirring occasionally. Season with a little salt and cayenne pepper.

2 Transfer the tomato mixture to a small food processor or blender, add 30ml/2 tbsp of the parsley and the orange juice and blend to form a smooth purée.

3 Preheat the grill (broiler) with the shelf at its highest. Arrange four curved scallop shells, or flameproof ramekin dishes, on a baking tray.

4 Heat 25g/1oz/2 tbsp of the butter in a small frying pan and fry the scallops, for about 2 minutes, or until sealed but not cooked through.

5 Pour the anis spirit into a ladle and set light to it. Pour over the scallops and shake the pan gently until the flames die down. Divide the scallops among the prepared shells (or dishes) and salt them lightly. Add the pan juices to the tomato sauce.

6 Pour the tomato sauce over the scallops. Mix together the breadcrumbs and the remaining parsley, season and sprinkle over the top.

7 Melt the remaining butter and drizzle over the breadcrumbs. Grill (broil) the scallops for about 1 minute to colour the tops and heat through. Serve immediately.

Serves 4

30ml/2 tbsp olive oil
1 onion, finely chopped
2 garlic cloves, finely chopped
200g/7oz can tomatoes
pinch of cayenne pepper
45ml/3 tbsp finely chopped
    fresh parsley
50ml/2fl oz/¼ cup orange juice
50g/2oz/4 tbsp butter
450g/1lb large shelled scallops,
    or 8–12 large ones on the shell,
    detached and cleaned
30ml/2 tbsp anis spirit, such as
    Ricard or Pernod
90ml/6 tbsp stale breadcrumbs
salt and ground black pepper

Scallops are the symbol of St James (Santiago), and this dish is associated with his shrine at Santiago de Compostella in Galicia. The flamed scallops are covered in tomato sauce and are served hot in the curved shell, with crisp breadcrumbs on top.

Navarra-style Trout
Truchas a la Navarra

1 Extend the belly cavity of each trout, cutting up along the length of one side of the backbone. Slip a knife behind the rib bones to loosen them (sometimes just flexing the fish makes them pop up). Snip these off from both sides with scissors, and season the fish well inside.

2 Preheat the grill (broiler) to high, with a shelf in the top position. Line a baking tray with foil and butter it.

3 Working with the fish on the foil, fold a piece of ham into each belly. Use smaller or broken bits of ham for this, and reserve the eight most complete slices.

4 Brush each trout with a little butter, seasoning the outside lightly with salt and pepper. Wrap two ham slices round each one, crossways, tucking the ends into the belly. Grill (broil) the trout for 4 minutes, then carefully turn them over with a metal spatula, rolling them across on the belly, so the ham doesn't come loose, and grill for a further 4 minutes.

5 Serve the trout very hot, with any spare butter spooned over the top. Diners should open the trout on their plates, and eat them from the inside, pushing the flesh off the skin.

Serves 4

4 brown or rainbow trout, about
    250g/9oz each, cleaned
50g/2oz/¼ cup melted butter, plus
    extra for greasing
16 thin slices Serrano ham, about
    200g/7oz
salt and ground black pepper
buttered potatoes, to serve (optional)

Traditionally, the trout would have come from mountain streams and been stuffed and wrapped in locally cured ham. One of the beauties of this method is that the skin comes off in one piece, leaving the succulent, moist flesh to be eaten with the crisped, salt ham.

Pan-fried Sole with Lemon and Capers
Lenguado con Limón y Alcaparras

Serves 2

30–45ml/2–3 tbsp plain
   (all-purpose) flour
4 sole, plaice or flounder fillets,
   or 2 whole small flat fish
45ml/3 tbsp olive oil
25g/1oz/2 tbsp butter
60ml/4 tbsp lemon juice
30ml/2 tbsp pickled capers, drained
salt and ground black pepper
fresh flat leaf parsley, to garnish
lemon wedges, to serve

1 Sift the flour on to a plate and season well with salt and ground black pepper. Dip the fish fillets into the flour, to coat evenly on both sides.

2 Heat the oil and butter in a large shallow pan until foaming. Add the fish fillets and fry over a medium heat for 2–3 minutes on each side.

3 Lift out the fillets carefully with a metal spatula and place them on a warmed serving platter. Season with salt and ground black pepper.

4 Add the lemon juice and capers to the pan, heat through and pour over the fish. Garnish with parsley and serve at once with lemon wedges.

COOK'S TIP

This is a flavourful, and quick, way to serve the fillets of any white fish. The delicate flavour is enhanced by the tangy lemon juice and capers.

Flat fish of different sorts abound in the Mediterranean and are usually fried simply and served with lemon wedges to squeeze over the top. Intensely flavoured capers, which grow extensively in the Balearic Islands, make a pleasant tangy addition.

Marinated Sardines
Sardinas en Escabeche

1 Using a sharp knife, cut the heads off the sardines and split each of them along the belly. Turn the fish over so that the backbone is uppermost. Press down along the entire backbone to loosen it, then carefully lift out the backbone and as many of the remaining little bones as possible.

2 Close the sardines up again and dust them with seasoned flour.

3 Heat the olive oil in a frying pan and fry the sardines for 2–3 minutes on each side. With a metal spatula, remove the fish from the pan to a plate and allow to cool, then pack them together in a single layer in a large shallow dish.

4 To make the marinade, add the olive oil to the oil remaining in the frying pan. Fry the onion and garlic gently for 5–10 minutes until soft and translucent, stirring occasionally. Add the bay leaves, cloves, chilli and paprika, with pepper to taste. Fry, stirring frequently, for another 1–2 minutes.

5 Stir in the vinegar, wine and a little salt. Allow to bubble up, then pour over the sardines. The marinade should cover the fish completely. When the fish is cool, cover and chill overnight or for up to three days. Serve the sardines and their marinade, garnished with the roasted onion, pepper and tomatoes.

Serves 2–4

12–16 sardines, cleaned
seasoned plain (all-purpose) flour,
    for dusting
30ml/2 tbsp olive oil
roasted red onion, green (bell) pepper
    and tomatoes, to garnish

For the marinade

90ml/6 tbsp olive oil
1 onion, sliced
1 garlic clove, crushed
3–4 bay leaves
2 cloves
1 dried red chilli, seeded and
    chopped
5ml/1 tsp paprika
120ml/4fl oz/½ cup wine
    or sherry vinegar
120ml/4fl oz/½ cup white wine
salt and ground black pepper

The Arabs invented marinades as a means of preserving poultry, meat and game, and escabeche *means "acid" in Arabic. In Spain this method was enthusiastically adopted as a means of keeping fish fresh. The fish are always fried first and then stored in vinegar.*

Chicken with Rice
Arroz con Pollo

Serves 4

60ml/4 tbsp olive oil

6 chicken thighs, free-range if possible, halved along the bone

5ml/1 tsp paprika

1 large Spanish onion, roughly chopped

2 garlic cloves, finely chopped

1 chorizo sausage, sliced

115g/4oz Serrano or cooked ham or gammon, diced

1 red (bell) pepper, seeded and roughly chopped

1 yellow (bell) pepper, seeded and roughly chopped

225g/8oz/1 generous cup paella rice, washed and drained

2 large tomatoes, chopped or 200g/7oz can chopped tomatoes

120ml/4fl oz/½ cup amontillado sherry

750ml/1¼ pints/3 cups chicken stock

5ml/1 tsp dried oregano or thyme

1 bay leaf

salt and ground black pepper

15 green olives and chopped fresh flat leaf parsley, to garnish

1 Heat the oil in a wide flameproof casserole. Season the chicken pieces with salt and paprika. Fry gently until nicely brown all over, then reserve on a plate.

2 Add the onion and garlic to the pan and fry gently until beginning to soften. Add the chorizo and ham or gammon and stir-fry. Add the chopped peppers. Cook until they begin to soften.

3 Sprinkle in the drained rice and cook, stirring, for 1–2 minutes. Add the tomatoes, sherry, chicken stock and dried herbs and season to taste. Arrange the chicken pieces deep in the mixture, and tuck in the bay leaf.

4 Cover and cook over a very low heat for 30–40 minutes, until the chicken and rice are done. Stir, then garnish and serve, sprinkled with chopped fresh flat leaf parsley.

Many Spanish families eat rice once a week, referring to it as arroz unless it is paella. Rice with chicken is a casserole, with more liquid than a paella. Seasonal vegetables are included and even peas and sweetcorn can be used.

Chicken Casserole with Spiced Figs
Estofado de Pollo con Higos

Serves 4

50g/2oz bacon lardons or pancetta,
    diced
15ml/1 tbsp olive oil
1.3–1.6kg/3–3½lb free-range or
    corn-fed chicken, jointed into
    eight pieces
120ml/4fl oz/½ cup white wine
finely pared rind (zest) of ½ lemon
50ml/2fl oz/¼ cup chicken stock
salt and ground black pepper
green salad, to serve

For the figs

150g/5oz/¾ cup sugar
120ml/4fl oz/½ cup white wine
    vinegar
1 lemon slice
1 cinnamon stick
120ml/4fl oz/½ cup water
450g/1lb fresh figs

*Here this flavoursome
chicken dish is cooked with
a beautifully spiced sauce,
which goes perfectly with
a Catalan Cabernet
Sauvignon.*

1 Prepare the figs. Simmer the sugar, vinegar, lemon and cinnamon with the water for 5 minutes. Add the figs and cook for 10 minutes. Remove from the heat and leave to stand for 3 hours, then drain and set aside.

2 Fry the bacon or pancetta until golden. Transfer to an ovenproof dish. Add the oil to the pan. Season the chicken, brown on both sides, then transfer to the ovenproof dish.

3 Preheat the oven to 180°C/350°F/Gas 4. Add the wine and lemon rind to the pan and boil until the wine has reduced and is syrupy. Pour over the chicken.

4 Cook the chicken in the oven, uncovered, for about 20 minutes, then add the figs and chicken stock. Cover and return to the oven for a further 10 minutes. Serve with a green salad.

Partridge with Grapes
Perdices con Uvas

Serves 4

4 partridges, cleaned
500g/1¼lb red grapes, split and
    seeded, plus extra to garnish
45–60ml/3–4 tbsp olive oil
4 rashers (slices) smoked streaky
    (fatty) bacon, halved across
1 onion, chopped
2 garlic cloves, finely chopped
1 bay leaf
120ml/4fl oz/½ cup dry white wine
250ml/8fl oz/1 cup game or
    chicken stock
salt and ground black pepper
steamed cabbage, to serve

1 Season the birds inside and out, then stuff with 250g/9oz grapes. Put 45ml/3 tbsp oil in a flameproof casserole. Fry the bacon until crisp, then reserve on a plate. Put the birds into the casserole breast sides down and fry until coloured. Turn them until brown all over. Remove.

2 Fry the onion and garlic, adding a little more oil if needed, until softened. Return the birds to the casserole and arrange two pieces of bacon on top of each. Push 125g/5oz grapes in around them, and add the bay leaf. Pour in the white wine and stock. Add plenty of black pepper. Simmer, covered, for 30 minutes.

3 Remove the birds and bacon to a plate. Spoon the casserole contents into a food processor, discard the bay leaf, and purée. Season.

4 Return the birds to the pan, pour the sauce around them, and add 125g/5oz grapes. Heat through. Garnish with extra grapes and crumbled bacon and serve with steamed cabbage.

Partridges are Spain's commonest game birds. They have a natural affinity with grapes, as wild birds often attack the harvest. Game hens or any plump small bird can be used for this pot roast.

Chorizo with Chestnuts Chorizos y Castañas

Serves 3–6

15ml/1 tbsp olive oil
4 red chorizo sausages, sliced
200g/7oz/1¼ cups peeled
    cooked chestnuts
15ml/1 tbsp paprika
salt and ground black pepper
crusty bread, to serve

1 Heat the oil in a wide frying pan and put in the chorizo slices in a single layer. Cook the chorizo for 3–4 minutes, turning frequently, until it starts to give off its oil.

2 Tip in the peeled chestnuts and toss until warm and covered with the chorizo oil. Add the paprika and season with salt and ground black pepper. Serve hot with crusty bread.

Chestnuts are native to Galicia and are a popular addition to many dishes. Chorizos y castanas makes a good side dish for roast turkey and a tasty supper dish served on its own.

Meatballs in Tomato Sauce
Albóndigas

Serves 4

225g/8oz minced (ground) beef
4 spring onions (scallions),
    thinly sliced
2 garlic cloves, finely chopped
30ml/2 tbsp grated fresh
    Parmesan cheese
10ml/2 tsp fresh thyme leaves
15ml/1 tbsp olive oil
3 tomatoes, chopped
30ml/2 tbsp red or dry white wine
10ml/2 tsp chopped fresh rosemary
pinch of sugar
salt and ground black pepper
fresh thyme, to garnish

1 Put the minced beef in a bowl. Add the spring onions, garlic, Parmesan and thyme and plenty of salt and pepper. Stir well to combine, then shape the mixture into 12 small firm balls.

2 Heat the olive oil in a large, heavy frying pan and cook the meatballs for about 5 minutes, turning frequently, until evenly browned all over.

3 Add the chopped tomatoes, wine, rosemary and sugar to the pan, with salt and ground black pepper to taste.

4 Cover the pan and cook gently for about 15 minutes until the tomatoes are pulpy and the meatballs are cooked through. Check the sauce for seasoning and serve the meatballs hot, garnished with the thyme.

Meatballs appear on many tapas menus. They make a substantial supper, too, with a green salad or pasta.

Mixed Meat Casserole Cocido

Serves 8

500–800g/1¼–1¾lb cured brisket
  or silverside (pot roast)
250g/9oz smoked streaky (fatty)
  bacon, in one piece, or 250g/9oz
  belly pork
1 knuckle gammon (smoked or cured
  ham) bone, with some meat
  still attached
500–750g/1¼–1¾lb beef marrow
  bone, sawn through
1 pig's trotter (foot), sawn through
1 whole garlic bulb
2 bay leaves
5ml/1 tsp black peppercorns,
  lightly crushed
250g/9oz/1¼ cups dried chickpeas,
  soaked overnight and drained
2 quarters corn-fed chicken
1 small onion, studded with
  2 or 3 cloves
2 large carrots, cut into big pieces
2 leeks, cut into chunks
500g/1¼lb small new potatoes,
  scrubbed
2 red chorizo sausages
1 *morcilla* or 250g/9oz black pudding
  (blood sausage)
30ml/2 tbsp long grain rice
1 small (bell) pepper, finely diced
salt

1 Put the salt meat – brisket or silverside, bacon or pork and knuckle – into a large pan and cover with water. Bring slowly to the boil, simmer for 5 minutes to remove excess salt, and drain.

2 Using a very large stockpot (with a capacity of at least 6 litres/10 pints/5 quarts), pack in all the meat, skin side down, with the marrow bone and trotter. Add the garlic bulb, bay leaves and peppercorns, with water to cover. Bring to simmering point, skimming off any scum, with a slotted spoon.

3 Add the chickpeas, cover and simmer on the lowest possible heat for 1½ hours, checking occasionally that there is enough liquid. Add the chicken and onion to the pot. Cook until the chickpeas are done.

4 Start the vegetables. Put the carrots, leeks and potatoes into a large pan with the chorizo (but not the *morcilla* or black pudding). Cover with water and bring to the boil. Simmer for 25 minutes, until the potatoes are cooked. 5 minutes before the end, add the *morcilla* or black pudding.

5 Strain off enough broth from the meat pot into a pan, for soup. Bring back to the boil, sprinkle in the rice and cook for 15 minutes. Add the pepper and cook for 2–3 minutes. Serve the soup as the first course.

6 Drain the vegetables and sausages and arrange on a platter. Serve as a separate second course or as an accompaniment with the meat. Slice the meats, removing the marrow from the bone and adding it to the chickpeas. Arrange with all the meats on a heated serving platter, moistening with a little broth.

The Spanish national dish, cocido is also Madrid's most famous stew. Simply meaning "boiled dinner" it consists of a pot of fresh and salt meat with chicken and sausages simmered with chickpeas and some fresh vegetables.

Lamb with Red Peppers and Rioja
Cordero con Pimientos y Rioja

Serves 4

15ml/1 tbsp plain (all-purpose) flour
1kg/2¼lb lean lamb, cubed
60ml/4 tbsp olive oil
2 red onions, sliced
4 garlic cloves, sliced
10ml/2 tsp paprika
1.5ml/¼ tsp ground cloves
400ml/14fl oz/1⅔ cups red Rioja
150ml/¼ pint/⅔ cup lamb stock
2 bay leaves
2 thyme sprigs
3 red (bell) peppers, halved
    and seeded
salt and ground black pepper
bay leaves and thyme sprigs,
    to garnish (optional)

World-famous for its red wine, Rioja also produces excellent red peppers. It even has a red pepper fair, at Lodoso, every year. Together they give this lamb stew a lovely rich flavour. Boiled potatoes make a very good accompaniment.

1 Preheat the oven to 160°C/325°F/Gas 3. Season the flour, add the lamb and toss lightly to coat.

2 Heat the oil in a frying pan and fry the lamb until browned all over. Transfer to an ovenproof dish. Fry the onions and garlic until soft. Add to the meat.

3 Add the paprika, cloves, Rioja, lamb stock, bay leaves and thyme and bring the mixture to a gentle simmer. Add the halved red peppers. Cover the dish with a lid or foil and cook for about 30 minutes, or until the meat is tender. Garnish with more bay leaves and sprigs of thyme, if you like.

Sirloin Steak with Blue Cheese Sauce
Solomillo con Cabrales

Serves 4

25g/1oz/2 tbsp butter
30ml/2 tbsp olive oil
4 fillet steaks (beef tenderloin), cut
   5cm/2in thick, about 150g/5oz
   each
salt and coarsely ground black
   pepper
roast vegetables, to serve

For the blue cheese sauce

30ml/2 tbsp Spanish brandy
150ml/5fl oz/⅔ cup double
   (heavy) cream
75g/3oz *Cabrales* or Roquefort
   cheese, crumbled

Well-hung beef is a feature of the Basque country, served here with Cabrales, the blue cheese from Spain's northern mountains. French Roquefort is also extremely popular, because it appeals to the Spanish love of salty flavours.

1 Heat the butter and oil together in a heavy frying pan, over a high heat. Season the steaks well. Fry them for just 2 minutes on each side, to sear them.

2 Lower the heat slightly and cook for a further 2–3 minutes on each side, or according to your taste. Remove the steaks to a warm plate.

3 To make the sauce, reduce the heat and add the brandy to the pan, stirring to pick up the juices. Add the cream and boil to reduce a little.

4 Add the crumbled cheese and mash it into the sauce using a spoon. Taste for seasoning. Serve in a small sauce jug (pitcher), or poured over the steaks. Serve with roast vegetables.

Veal Casserole with Broad Beans
Cazuela de Ternera con Habas

Serves 6
45ml/3 tbsp olive oil
1.3–1.6kg/3–3½lb veal, cut into
    5cm/2in cubes
1 large onion, chopped
6 large garlic cloves, unpeeled
1 bay leaf
5ml/1 tsp paprika
240ml/8fl oz/1 cup fino sherry
100g/4oz/scant 1 cup shelled,
    skinned broad (fava) beans
60ml/4 tbsp chopped fresh flat
    leaf parsley
salt and ground black pepper

1 Heat 30ml/2 tbsp oil in a large flameproof casserole. Add half the meat and brown well on all sides. Transfer to a plate. Brown the rest of the meat and remove from the pan.

2 Add the remaining oil to the pan and cook the onion until soft. Return the meat to the casserole and stir well to mix with the onion.

3 Add the garlic cloves, bay leaf, paprika and sherry. Season with salt and black pepper. Bring to simmering point, then cover and cook very gently for 30–40 minutes.

4 Add the broad beans to the casserole about 10 minutes before the end of the cooking time. Check the seasoning and stir in the chopped parsley just before serving.

This delicate stew, flavoured with sherry and plenty of garlic, is a spring dish made with new vegetables – menestra de ternera. For a delicious flavour be sure to add plenty of parsley just before serving. Lamb is equally good cooked in this way.

Baked Custard Flan

1 Select your moulds – eight metal dariole moulds, about 120ml/4fl oz/½ cup each, or a soufflé dish 1 litre/13¾ pints/4 cups in capacity. Arrange in a roasting pan.

2 Put 175g/6oz/⅞ cup of the sugar in a small heavy pan with 60ml/4 tbsp water. Bring to the boil over a high heat, swirling the pan to dissolve the sugar. Boil, without stirring, for about 5 minutes until the syrup turns a dark caramel colour.

3 If using individual moulds, pour a little caramel into each one. If using a single mould, lift it with oven gloves and quickly swirl the dish to coat the base with the caramel. (The caramel will harden quickly as it cools.)

4 Preheat the oven to 160°C/325°F/Gas 3. If using, split the vanilla pod lengthways and scrape out the seeds. Pour the milk and cream into a pan, add the vanilla seeds or extract and bring the mixture close to the boil, stirring. Remove from the heat and allow to stand for 15–20 minutes.

5 In a bowl, whisk the eggs and extra yolks with the remaining sugar for 2–3 minutes until creamy. Whisk in the warm milk and cream mixture, and then strain it into the caramel-lined mould(s). Cover with foil.

6 Pour boiling water into the pan, to come halfway up the sides of the mould(s). Bake until the custard is just set (20–25 minutes for small moulds; about 40 minutes for a large one). To test that the custard has set, a knife inserted into the custard should come out clean. Remove from the water, leave to cool, then chill overnight.

7 To turn out, run a palette knife around the custard(s). Cover a large mould with a serving dish and, holding tightly, invert the dish and plate together. Lift one edge of the mould, waiting for the caramel to run down, then remove the mould. Cover the small moulds with saucers and invert them to serve.

Serves 8

250g/9oz/1¼ cups caster (superfine) sugar
1 vanilla pod (bean) or 10ml/2 tsp vanilla extract
400ml/14fl oz/1⅔ cups milk
250ml/8fl oz/1 cup whipping cream
5 large (US extra large) eggs
2 egg yolks

These little baked caramel custards, made in bucket-shaped moulds, are the best-known and most popular of all Spanish desserts. If you don't own small moulds, you can make one large flan instead but it will need to be cooked for a little longer.

Crème Brûlée Crema Catalana

Serves 4

475ml/16fl oz/2 cups milk
pared rind (zest) of ½ lemon
1 cinnamon stick
4 large egg yolks
105ml/7 tbsp caster (superfine)
    sugar
25ml/1½ tbsp cornflour (cornstarch)
ground nutmeg, for sprinkling

*This fabulous Spanish
dessert of creamy custard,
topped with a net of brittle
sugar, may well be the
original of all crème brûlées.
Cremat is the Catalan
word for "burnt", and this
was probably part of its
original name.*

1 Put the milk in a pan with the lemon rind and cinnamon stick. Bring to the boil, then simmer for 10 minutes. Remove the lemon rind and cinnamon. Put the egg yolks and 45ml/3 tbsp sugar in a bowl, and whisk until pale yellow. Add the cornflour and mix well.

2 Stir a few tablespoons of the hot milk into the egg yolk mixture, then tip back into the remaining milk. Return to the heat and cook gently, stirring, for about 5 minutes, until thickened and smooth. Do not boil.

3 Pour the custard into four shallow ovenproof dishes, about 13cm/5in in diameter. Leave to cool, then chill for a few hours until firm.

4 No more than 30 minutes before serving, sprinkle each dessert with 15ml/1 tbsp of the sugar and a little nutmeg. Preheat the grill (broiler) to high. Place the dishes under the grill, on the highest shelf, and cook until the sugar caramelizes. Take care as this will only take a few seconds and it will caramelize unevenly. Leave the custards to cool for a few minutes before serving.

Poor Knights Torrijas

Serves 4

120ml/4fl oz/½ cup white wine
12 thick rounds of stale crusty bread
2 large eggs
60–90ml/4–6 tbsp sunflower oil
ground cinnamon, and caster
    (superfine) sugar, for dusting

1 Pour the wine into a shallow dish and dip the bread rounds into it.

2 Beat the eggs together in another shallow dish. Dip half the bread rounds into the beaten egg on each side so that they are completely covered.

3 Heat 60ml/4 tbsp oil in a pan until very hot and fry the bread rounds for about 1 minute on each side until crisp and golden. Reserve on kitchen paper, then dip and fry the rest, adding more oil if necessary. Serve hot, sprinkled with cinnamon and sugar.

COOK'S TIP
These toasts are often enjoyed at festivals and are a typical dish from Madrid (although variations can be found all over Europe). Milk can be used in place of white wine, if liked, making them suitable for children.

Translated as "poor knights", these sugared toasts are perfect for almost every occasion. Made with milk, they make a good tea-time snack for children, or to accompany a cup of hot chocolate. As a dessert they are the equivalent of France's toasted brioche – an accompaniment to ice cream, or to any baked fruit. They are also very popular by themselves.

Honey Fritters Pestiños

1 Preheat the oven to 190°C/375°F/Gas 5. Sift the flour on to a sheet of baking parchment. Heat the oil in a small pan with the crushed aniseed, until the aniseed releases its aroma. Strain the oil into a larger pan and add the sugar, water and anisette. Heat to a rolling boil.

2 Remove the pan from the heat and add the sifted flour, all in one go. Beat vigorously with a wooden spoon until the mixture leaves the sides of the pan clean. Leave to cool.

3 Meanwhile lightly beat the eggs. Gradually incorporate the egg into the dough mixture, beating hard. You may not need to use all the egg – the paste should be soft but not sloppy. Reserve any remaining beaten egg to glaze the fritters.

4 Grease and flour two baking sheets. Fit a plain nozzle to a piping (pastry) bag and pipe small rounds of dough about 2.5cm/1in across on the sheets, spacing them about 2.5cm/1in apart. Brush with the remaining beaten egg.

5 Bake for about 30 minutes, or until lightly brown and an even texture right through. (Lift one off the sheet to test.)

6 To make the syrup, melt the honey in a small pan and stir in the anisette. Just before serving, use a slotted spoon to dunk the pestiños into the syrup.

The Arabs invented all sorts of sweet bites, to eat after the main course or with drinks. Bathed in scented honey syrup, pestiños were often deep-fried and known as dulces de sárten, which means "sweets from the frying pan". However, at home it is a good deal easier to bake them and they puff up beautifully in the oven.

Makes about 30

225g/8oz/2 cups plain (all-purpose) flour, plus extra for dusting
60ml/4 tbsp sunflower oil
15ml/1 tbsp aniseed, lightly crushed
45ml/3 tbsp caster (superfine) sugar
250ml/8fl oz/1 cup water
60ml/4 tbsp anisette
3 small (US medium) eggs

For the anis syrup

60ml/4 tbsp clear honey
60ml/4 tbsp anisette

COOK'S TIP

Anisette is a sweet aniseed liqueur that gives the syrup a wonderful flavour. If you cannot find anisette, use another anis spirit such as Ricard instead.

Festival Cakes Panellets

Makes about 24

115g/4oz sweet potato, peeled
butter, for greasing
1 large (US extra large) egg,
    separated
225g/8oz/2 cups ground almonds
200g/7oz/1 cup caster (superfine)
    sugar, plus extra for sprinkling
finely grated rind (zest) of 1 small
    lemon
7.5ml/1½ tsp vanilla extract
60ml/4 tbsp pine nuts
60ml/4 tbsp pistachio nuts, chopped

The Catalan name for these nutty festival cakes means "little bread", but they are, in fact, much closer to marzipan, with a slightly soft centre that is produced by their secret ingredient – sweet potato. Patisseries make hundreds of these little cakes for All Saints' Day, on 1st November, when families take flowers to the graveyards.

1 Dice the sweet potato, and cook it in a pan of boiling water for 15 minutes, or until soft. Drain and leave to cool. Preheat the oven to 200°C/400°F/Gas 6. Line a baking sheet with foil and grease with butter.

2 Put the cooled sweet potato in a food processor and process to make a smooth purée, then work in the egg yolk, ground almonds, sugar, lemon rind and vanilla extract to make a soft dough. Transfer the dough to a bowl and chill for 30 minutes.

3 Spoon walnut-sized balls of dough on to the foil, spacing them about 2.5cm/1in apart, then flatten them out slightly.

4 Lightly beat the egg white and brush over the cakes. Sprinkle half the cakes with pine nuts, and half with pistachio nuts. Sprinkle lightly with sugar and bake for 10 minutes, or until lightly browned. Leave to cool on the foil, then lift off with a metal spatula.

Nutritional notes

Olive and Anchovy Bites: Energy 42kcal/173kJ; Protein 1.2g; Carbohydrate 2g, of which sugars 0.1g; Fat 3.2g, of which saturates 1.9g; Cholesterol 9mg; Calcium 27mg; Fibre 0.1g; Sodium 103mg.

Beetroot Crisps: Energy 155kcal/639kJ; Protein 0.3g; Carbohydrate 1.4g, of which sugars 1.3g; Fat 16.5g, of which saturates 2.4g; Cholesterol 0mg; Calcium 4mg; Fibre 0.4g; Sodium 13mg.

Potatoes in Spicy Sauce: Energy 256kcal/1070kJ; Protein 3.3g; Carbohydrate 30g, of which sugars 4.9g; Fat 14.4g, of which saturates 2.2g; Cholesterol 0mg; Calcium 14mg; Fibre 2.4g; Sodium 20mg.

Garlic Prawns: Energy 170kcal/705kJ; Protein 9g; Carbohydrate 1g, of which sugars 0g; Fat 15g, of which saturates 5g; Cholesterol 122mg; Calcium 53mg; Fibre 0g; Sodium 438mg.

Moorish Skewers: Energy 233kcal/970kJ; Protein 27g; Carbohydrate 0.7g, of which sugars 0g; Fat 13.5g, of which saturates 2.9g; Cholesterol 79mg; Calcium 25mg; Fibre 0.6g; Sodium 99mg.

Spicy Sausage and Cheese Tortilla: Energy 409kcal/1703kJ; Protein 14.9g; Carbohydrate 28.3g, of which sugars 6.8g; Fat 26.7g, of which saturates 9.5g; Cholesterol 157mg; Calcium 212mg; Fibre 2.7g; Sodium 438mg.

Chilled Tomato and Garlic Soup: Energy 376kcal/1584kJ; Protein 11.3g; Carbohydrate 38.3g, of which sugars 31.3g; Fat 21.1g, of which saturates 3.6g; Cholesterol 95mg; Calcium 109mg; Fibre 8.3g; Sodium 1032mg.

Sherried Onion Soup: Energy 246kcal/1017kJ; Protein 5.5g; Carbohydrate 9.5g, of which sugars 6.7g; Fat 19.6g, of which saturates 6.1g; Cholesterol 21mg; Calcium 76mg; Fibre 2.9g; Sodium 68mg.

Seafood Soup: Energy 301kcal/1266kJ; Protein 39.5g; Carbohydrate 13.5g, of which sugars 6.3g; Fat 10.3g, of which saturates 1.6g; Cholesterol 362mg; Calcium 223mg; Fibre 1.9g; Sodium 709mg.

Roast Peppers and Onions: Energy 75kcal/313kJ; Protein 1.3g; Carbohydrate 7.5g, of which sugars 7.2g; Fat 3.9g, of which saturates 0.6g; Cholesterol 0mg; Calcium 17mg; Fibre 2g; Sodium 151mg.

Broad Beans with Bacon: Energy 139kcal/577kJ; Protein 6.8g; Carbohydrate 8.2g, of which sugars 1.6g; Fat 9g, of which saturates 1.9g; Cholesterol 8mg; Calcium 38mg; Fibre 3.9g; Sodium 163mg.

Lentils with Mushrooms and Anis: Energy 242kcal/1018kJ; Protein 12.5g; Carbohydrate 29.8g, of which sugars 9.5g; Fat 7.2g, of which saturates 1g; Cholesterol 0mg; Calcium 83mg; Fibre 6.9g; Sodium 23mg.

Seafood Paella: Energy 585kcal/2445kJ; Protein 36.1g; Carbohydrate 60.9g, of which sugars 10.1g; Fat 20.4g, of which saturates 5.6g; Cholesterol 268mg; Calcium 132mg; Fibre 4.2g; Sodium 1055mg.

Scallops in Tomato Sauce: Energy 394kcal/ 1652kJ; Protein 29.7g; Carbohydrate 25.5g, of which sugars 4.4g; Fat 18.1g, of which saturates 7.8g; Cholesterol 80mg; Calcium 95mg; Fibre 1.8g; Sodium 459mg.

Navarra-style Trout: Energy 369kcal/1546kJ; Protein 48g; Carbohydrate 0.6g, of which sugars 0.6g; Fat 19.4g, of which saturates 8.8g; Cholesterol 216mg; Calcium 66mg; Fibre 0g; Sodium 821mg.

Pan-fried Sole: Energy 425kcal/1773kJ; Protein 34.2g; Carbohydrate 5.9g, of which sugars 0.2g; Fat 29.7g, of which saturates 9.3g; Cholesterol 111mg; Calcium 103mg; Fibre 0.3g; Sodium 316mg.

Marinated Sardines: Energy 242kcal/1004kJ; Protein 15.8g; Carbohydrate 1.7g, of which sugars 0.9g; Fat 18.1g, of which saturates 3.6g; Cholesterol 0mg; Calcium 70mg; Fibre 0.2g; Sodium 92mg.

Chicken with Rice: Energy 654kcal/2736kJ; Protein 49.7g; Carbohydrate 59.3g, of which sugars 11.2g; Fat 20.6g, of which saturates 5g; Cholesterol 132mg; Calcium 52mg; Fibre 2.8g; Sodium 651mg.

Chicken Casserole with Spiced Figs: Energy 811kcal/3396kJ; Protein 44g; Carbohydrate 69.8g, of which sugars 69.8g; Fat 39.2g, of which saturates 10.9g; Cholesterol 215mg; Calcium 183mg; Fibre 4.3g; Sodium 394mg.

Partridge with Grapes: Energy 932kcal/3908kJ; Protein 133.4g; Carbohydrate 17.4g, of which sugars 9.4g; Fat 30.9g, of which saturates 7.3g; Cholesterol 17mg; Calcium 219mg; Fibre 5.2g; Sodium 695mg.

Chorizo with Chestnuts: Energy 180kcal/752kJ; Protein 4.2g; Carbohydrate 17g, of which sugars 2.9g; Fat 11.1g, of which saturates 3.8g; Cholesterol 13mg; Calcium 36mg; Fibre 1.5g; Sodium 275mg.

Meatballs in Tomato Sauce: Energy 206kcal/856kJ; Protein 14.4g; Carbohydrate 5.2g, of which sugars 5.1g; Fat 13.8g, of which saturates 5.5g; Cholesterol 38mg; Calcium 121mg; Fibre 1.5g; Sodium 133mg.

Mixed Meat Casserole: Energy 593kcal/2478kJ; Protein 46.4g; Carbohydrate 37g, of which sugars 4.5g; Fat 29.6g, of which saturates 10.1g; Cholesterol 138mg; Calcium 116mg; Fibre 5.3g; Sodium 1100mg.

Lamb with Red Peppers and Rioja: Energy 635kcal/2646kJ; Protein 49.8g; Carbohydrate 4.1g, of which sugars 0.4g; Fat 39.4g, of which saturates 14.6g; Cholesterol 190mg; Calcium 37mg; Fibre 0.2g; Sodium 223mg.

Sirloin Steak with Cheese Sauce: Energy 573kcal/2374kJ; Protein 36.3g; Carbohydrate 0.7g, of which sugars 0.7g; Fat 45.4g, of which saturates 24.4g; Cholesterol 170mg; Calcium 117mg; Fibre 0g; Sodium 341mg.

Veal Casserole with Broad Beans: Energy 352kcal/1473kJ; Protein 47.4g; Carbohydrate 3.6g, of which sugars 1.3g; Fat 11.6g, of which saturates 2.8g; Cholesterol 182mg; Calcium 34mg; Fibre 1.2g; Sodium 244mg.

Baked Custard: Energy 332kcal/1394kJ; Protein 7g; Carbohydrate 42.3g, of which sugars 42.3g; Fat 16.3g, of which saturates 8.5g; Cholesterol 200mg; Calcium 119mg; Fibre 0g; Sodium 76mg.

Crème Brûlée: Energy 244kcal/1030kJ; Protein 7.2g; Carbohydrate 38.8g, of which sugars 33g; Fat 7.8g, of which saturates 2.9g; Cholesterol 217mg; Calcium 182mg; Fibre 0g; Sodium 65mg.

Poor Knights: Energy 419kcal/1763kJ; Protein 12.2g; Carbohydrate 56.3g, of which sugars 3g; Fat 15.7g, of which saturates 2.4g; Cholesterol 95mg; Calcium 138mg; Fibre 2.4g; Sodium 652mg.

Honey Fritters: Energy 65kcal/272kJ; Protein 1.3g; Carbohydrate 8.9g, of which sugars 3.2g; Fat 2.1g, of which saturates 0.3g; Cholesterol 19mg; Calcium 14mg; Fibre 0.2g; Sodium 8mg.

Festival Cakes: Energy 130kcal/541kJ; Protein 3.1g; Carbohydrate 10.7g, of which sugars 9.6g; Fat 8.6g, of which saturates 0.8g; Cholesterol 8mg; Calcium 32mg; Fibre 1g; Sodium 20mg.

Index